Healthy Eating with MyPyramid

Healthy Snacks

by Mari C. Schuh

Consulting Editor: Gail Saunders-Smith, PhD

Consultant: Barbara J. Rolls, PhD
Guthrie Chair in Nutrition
The Pennsylvania State University
University Park, Pennsylvania

Capstone
press

Mankato, Minnesota

Pebble Plus is published by Capstone Press,
151 Good Counsel Drive, P.O. Box 669, Mankato, Minnesota 56002.
www.capstonepress.com

1 2 3 4 5 6 11 10 09 08 07 06

Library of Congress Cataloging-in-Publication Data
Schuh, Mari C., 1975–
   Healthy Snacks / by Mari C. Schuh.
   p. cm.—(Pebble Plus. Healthy eating with MyPyramid)
   Summary: "Simple text and photographs present healthy snacks, examples of healthy snacks, and ways to
enjoy healthy snacks"—Provided by publisher.
   Includes bibliographical references and index.
   ISBN-13: 978-0-7368-5369-9 (hardcover)
   ISBN-10: 0-7368-5369-3 (hardcover)
   1. Snack foods—Juvenile literature. 2. Nutrition—Juvenile literature. I. Title. II. Series.
TX740.S3258 2006
641.5'39—dc22   2005023713

Credits
 Jennifer Bergstrom, designer; Kelly Garvin, photo researcher; Stacy Foster, photo shoot coordinator

Photo Credits
Capstone Press/Karon Dubke, all except U.S. Department of Agriculture, 8 (inset), 9 (computer screen)

Capstone Press thanks Hilltop Hy-Vee employees in Mankato, Minnesota, for their helpful assistance with
photo shoots.

The author dedicates this book to her brothers, John and Ryan Schuh.

**Information in this book supports the U.S. Department of Agriculture's MyPyramid for Kids
food guidance system found at http://www.MyPyramid.gov/kids.**

**The U.S. Department of Agriculture (USDA) does not endorse any products, services,
or organizations.**

Note to Parents and Teachers

The Healthy Eating with MyPyramid set supports national science standards related to
nutrition and physical health. This book describes and illustrates healthy snacks. The
images support early readers in understanding the text. The repetition of words and
phrases helps early readers learn new words. This book also introduces early readers
to subject-specific vocabulary words, which are defined in the Glossary section. Early
readers may need assistance to read some words and to use the Table of Contents,
Glossary, Read More, Internet Sites, and Index sections of the book.

Table of Contents

Healthy Snacks

Snacks are foods you eat
when you are hungry
between meals.
Small healthy snacks
help you grow strong.

A healthy snack gives you
energy until your next meal.
What snacks have you
eaten today?

MyPyramid for Kids

Learn more about healthy snacks and healthy eating from MyPyramid. MyPyramid is a tool to help you eat healthy food.

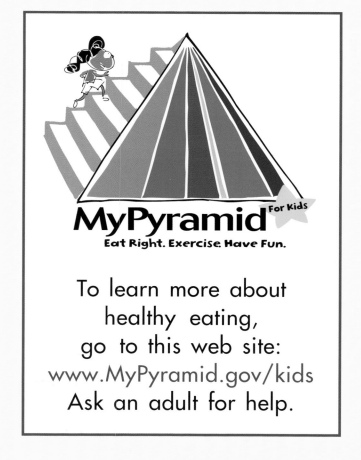

MyPyramid For Kids

Eat Right. Exercise. Have Fun.

To learn more about
healthy eating,
go to this web site:
www.MyPyramid.gov/kids
Ask an adult for help.

MyPyramid shows you
all the food groups.
You can choose
healthy snacks
from every food group.

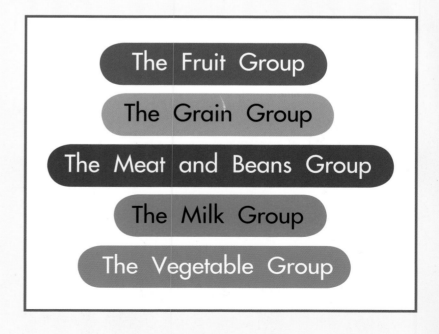

The Fruit Group

The Grain Group

The Meat and Beans Group

The Milk Group

The Vegetable Group

11

Enjoying Healthy Snacks

Got the munchies?

A small bowl

of low-fat popcorn makes

a great afternoon snack.

Mmmm! Carrots and celery taste yummy dipped in salad dressing. What's your favorite vegetable snack?

Are you thirsty?
Make a smoothie
with your favorite yogurt
and fruit. Gulp!

Nibble, nibble, nibble.

Whole-wheat crackers

topped with cheese

can fill you up.

It's easy and fun
to make healthy snacks.
Healthy food fuels your body.
Enjoy!

Healthy Snack Ideas

If you have the munchies between meals, eat a small healthy snack. Small snacks will fuel your body until your next meal.

Try one of these foods the next time you get hungry between meals!

vegetable soup

fresh fruit

string cheese

carrots and low-fat dip

sliced orange

cherry tomatoes

cereal with fruit

sunflower seeds

Glossary

energy—the strength to be active without getting tired

MyPyramid—a food plan that helps kids make healthy food choices and reminds kids to be active; MyPyramid was created by the U.S. Department of Agriculture.

smoothie—a thick, smooth drink made by mixing ice, milk or juice, low-fat yogurt, and fruit in a blender

snack—a small amount of food people eat when they are hungry between meals

Read More

Gray, Shirley Wimbish. *Eating for Good Health.* Living Well. Chanhassen, Minn.: Child's World, 2004.

Kalman, Bobbie. *Super Snacks.* Kid Power. New York: Crabtree, 2003.

Slazmann, Mary Elizabeth. *Eating Right.* Healthy Habits. Edina, Minn.: Abdo, 2004.

Index

Word Count: 138
Grade: 1
Early-Intervention Level: 14

Internet Sites

FactHound offers a safe, fun way to find Internet sites related to this book. All of the sites on FactHound have been researched by our staff.

Here's how:

1. Visit *www.facthound.com*

2. Type in this special code **0736853693** for age-appropriate sites. Or enter a search word related to this book for a more general search.

3. Click on the **Fetch It** button.

FactHound will fetch the best sites for you!